Psychology Child

Alexa Murphy

Copyright Page

Copyright Holder: © 2024, Andrea Jimenez
Year: 2024
Author: © 2024, Alexa Murph

Legal and Copyright Information

Index

Introduction to Child Psychology

Child psychology is a branch of psychology that studies how children think, feel, and behave from birth through adolescence. For parents, understanding these processes is like having a map that guides them on the path of parenting. Each child is a unique world, but there are development patterns that, when known, allow us to help children grow in a healthy and happy way. In this chapter, we will explore how child psychology can become a fundamental tool to be better parents and guide our children in their first years of life.

From the moment they are born, children begin a constant process of learning and adapting to the world around them. As parents, our role is to accompany them in this process, offering the emotional support and resources necessary for them to develop their personality and skills. Child psychology helps us understand that children are not small adults, but rather beings in full development. Their brains, emotions and behaviors evolve as they grow, and each stage has its own characteristics that we must know in order to guide them correctly.

For example, it's common for a young child to have tantrums or get frustrated easily. Rather than seeing it as a problem of bad behavior, child psychology teaches us that these reactions are a natural part of emotional development. Children don't yet know how to manage their emotions effectively, and those outbursts of crying or anger are their way of expressing that something isn't right for them. If we understand this, we can approach them with more patience and look for solutions that not only correct the behavior, but also teach them how to manage what they feel.

Another important aspect of child psychology is attachment. Studies have shown that the type of relationship children develop with their parents or caregivers in the early years of life has a profound impact on their future emotional health. A secure attachment, achieved through loving and consistent care, gives a child the confidence to safely explore the world. If a child feels protected and loved, they will have fewer fears and insecurities, leading them to develop healthy self-esteem. Understanding this motivates us to be more present and aware in our children's daily lives.

Child psychology also teaches us that the environment in which children grow up plays a fundamental role in their development. Children learn by observing the people around them. They imitate behaviors, absorb emotions, and are influenced by their environment. If a child grows up in an environment filled with love, respect, and understanding, they are likely to develop those same qualities. However, if the environment is marked by tension, conflict, or indifference, the child may grow up feeling insecure or having difficulty relating to others. This reminds us of the great responsibility we have as parents, not only in what we say, but also in how we act and how we live our own lives.

Over the years, child psychology has developed various techniques and theories that help us solve parenting challenges more effectively. For example, today, we know that physical or verbal punishment are not recommended ways to correct a child. Although they can stop a behavior immediately, in the long term, they can generate fears, resentments, and self-esteem problems. Instead, psychology offers us strategies such as positive discipline, which is based on teaching children through example, empathy, and the logical consequences of their actions. In this way, we not only correct, but we also help children understand why certain behaviors are not appropriate and how they can improve.

Understanding child psychology is like having a guide to interpret the signals that children give us, sometimes in confusing or subtle ways. It is not always easy to be a parent, but with the right knowledge, we can face challenges more calmly and effectively. It is not about being perfect, but about being willing to learn and adapt to the needs of our children. Just as they are constantly developing, we as parents are also learning and growing.

In short, child psychology invites us to view parenting from a broader and more conscious perspective. It shows us that parenting is much more than caring for children's physical needs; it is about understanding their inner world, their emotions and their thoughts. This knowledge allows us to accompany them in their growth in a more respectful and effective way, offering them the necessary tools for them to become healthy and happy adults. By knowing more about child development, we equip ourselves with the wisdom necessary to parent with love, understanding and patience, knowing that every small action has a lasting impact on the lives of our children.

Understanding Child Development

Child development is a fascinating and complex process. Children don't just grow in size, they also evolve mentally, emotionally and socially. Each stage of childhood is marked by important changes that influence the way children see the world, how they think and how they interact with the people around them. Understanding this development allows us to be more aware of what our children need at each moment, and how we can support them to grow in a balanced and happy way.

From birth, babies begin to explore the world through their senses. At first glance, it may seem like a newborn doesn't do much more than eat and sleep, but the reality is that their brains are constantly working. Babies observe their surroundings, hear voices, feel textures, and develop emotional bonds with the people who care for them. This first stage, called the sensorimotor stage, is crucial because it's where children begin to understand the relationship between their actions and outcomes. For example, they learn that when they cry, mom or dad will come to tend to their needs. These kinds of discoveries, even though they may seem small, are the foundation of their cognitive development.

As they grow, children enter the preoperational stage, which usually begins around age two. During this phase, children develop skills that change the way they interact with the world. One of the most important milestones of this stage is language development. Children begin to use words to describe what they see, feel, and want. Although their ideas may sometimes seem confusing or illogical to adults, this is a normal phase of development. At this stage, children cannot yet understand other people's point of view; they see the world from their perspective and often believe that others think and feel the same way they do. This is why they may seem selfish in certain situations, but they do not do so out of malice - they simply have not yet developed the ability to put themselves in other people's shoes.

During these preschool years, children also begin to experiment with symbolic play. This type of play is critical to their development, as it allows them to use their imagination to create situations and roles that help them understand the world. For example, they can pretend to be superheroes, doctors, or teachers, which not only entertains them, but also teaches them social skills and allows them to experiment with different emotions and scenarios. Through play, children learn to solve problems, negotiate with peers, and process emotions that they may not know how to express otherwise.

Around age seven, children enter what is known as the concrete operational stage. During this time, their thinking becomes more logical and organized. Children in this stage may begin to understand more complex concepts, such as quantity, time, and cause and effect. One significant change at this stage is that children no longer see everything from their own point of view. They begin to develop the ability to understand that other people have different thoughts, beliefs, and feelings than they do. This allows them to relate more effectively to others, and it is also the time when they begin to make more meaningful friends.

This stage is also a good time to introduce more abstract concepts, such as responsibility and empathy. Children no longer need to see or touch something to understand it; they can imagine situations, think of solutions, and make decisions based on the information they have. As their thinking becomes more mature, children also begin to better manage their emotions. Although they may still have moments of frustration or tantrums, they are increasingly able to identify what they are feeling and find ways to calm themselves down.

The final stage of child development is the formal operational stage, which begins in adolescence. This is when abstract thinking really takes off. Teens are no longer limited to what is tangible or immediate; they can think about complex ideas, such as justice, morality, and the future. They also begin to develop a more defined identity and question who they are and what they want to do with their lives. This is a crucial time in development, as teens seek independence while also needing support and guidance from their parents.

Each of these stages is an important piece in the puzzle of child development. What parents need to understand is that children do not move from one stage to the next overnight. Growth is gradual and there can sometimes be advances and setbacks. A child who seems very independent at one time, may become more dependent at another. This is completely normal and part of the process. Also, every child is different, and while some may reach certain milestones faster, others may need more time. There is no exact formula, and it is important not to compare children to one another.

For parents, knowing the stages of child development is essential because it helps them set realistic expectations. We can't expect a two-year-old to understand the same things as an eight-year-old, and we can't treat a teenager like a toddler either. Each stage has its own challenges, but also its rewards. The key is to be present, offer support, and foster an environment where children can explore, learn, and grow at their own pace.

In short, child development is an exciting journey full of discovery for both children and parents. Throughout this journey, patience, understanding and love are our best tools. By knowing how our children think and feel at each stage, we can offer them the right support to grow into confident, empathetic and happy individuals. Child development psychology gives us the map, but it is our caring and commitment that makes the journey meaningful for them.

The Importance of Attachment in Childhood

Attachment in infancy is one of the most important things in a child's development. It's not just about providing food and shelter, but about creating a deep emotional bond that makes them feel safe, loved and protected. This bond, known as attachment, is what will allow them to explore the world with confidence and learn to relate to others in a healthy way. From the moment a baby is born, they begin to seek the closeness of the people who care for them, and throughout the first years of life, this attachment becomes the foundation on which all their future relationships will be built.

Attachment begins when parents or caregivers respond to a baby's needs. If a baby cries, and his or her mom or dad comforts him or her, changes his or her diaper, or feeds him or her, the baby begins to understand that he or she can trust these people. This trust is key, since a child who feels secure is more likely to explore his or her environment, try new things, and learn without fear. On the other hand, if the child does not receive that adequate response, he or she may develop insecurities and become more fearful or anxious.

There are several types of attachment, but the most desirable is secure attachment. This type of attachment occurs when parents are available and consistently respond to the child's emotional and physical needs. A child with secure attachment knows that even if they wander off to explore or play, they can always return to a safe place: their parents' arms. This allows them to venture out and discover the world, but with the peace of mind that if something goes wrong, there will always be someone there to support them.

Throughout a child's life, this secure attachment becomes a kind of emotional "anchor." In situations of stress or fear, the child looks to his or her parents as a source of comfort. This doesn't mean that securely attached children never feel anxiety or sadness, but it does mean that they know they are not alone and that they have someone to rely on. This sense of constant support is not only critical during childhood, but it also influences how children will cope with life's challenges as they grow up.

Attachment also has a direct impact on a child's emotional development. Children who are securely attached are often better able to regulate their emotions. For example, if a securely attached child is feeling frustrated because they can't solve a problem, they are more likely to seek help or comfort rather than react aggressively or in despair. This is because they have learned, through their early experiences, that difficult emotions can be managed with the right support.

As children grow older and enter preschool, attachment continues to play an important role in their lives. A child with a secure attachment is more likely to relate well to peers, be empathetic, and be able to form more stable friendships. This is because attachment not only influences how a child sees his or her parents, but also how he or she sees the world. A child who feels loved and cared for learns to love and care for others.

However, not all children develop a secure attachment. In some cases, children may form what is called an insecure attachment. This occurs when parents or caregivers are inconsistent in their responses. For example, if a parent sometimes responds with affection and other times is distant or indifferent, the child may become confused and not know whether to trust that person. This can lead to the child becoming more dependent and anxious, or conversely, more distant and distrustful. In either case, an insecure attachment can hinder a child's emotional and social development.

Attachment also has a lasting impact on adult life. Studies have shown that adults who had a secure attachment in childhood tend to have healthier and more balanced relationships. This is because, by learning to trust and be trusted from a young age, they are able to form more stable bonds and better manage conflicts. In contrast, people with an insecure attachment in childhood may have more difficulty trusting others or maintaining healthy relationships.

It is important to note that attachment is not only formed in the first few months of life. Although the first few years are critical, parents always have the opportunity to strengthen or repair the bond with their children, even if there were difficulties in the past. The most important thing is consistency, affection and patience. Creating a secure attachment does not mean being a perfect parent, but rather being emotionally present, responsive to the child's needs and offering a safe space where they feel understood.

As children grow, the type of attachment they develop with their parents also influences how they handle difficult situations. A securely attached child will likely have a greater ability to cope with stress and adversity. This doesn't mean they won't feel sad, angry, or frustrated, but they have learned that difficult emotions can be overcome with the right support. Additionally, a secure attachment encourages independence. Contrary to popular belief, when children know they have a safe place to return to, they are more likely to venture out and seek new experiences on their own.

In conclusion, attachment in childhood is much more than just an emotional connection. It is the foundation on which a person's entire emotional, social and psychological life is built. A secure attachment allows children to develop in a balanced way, face the world with confidence and form healthy relationships throughout their lives. As parents, we must be attentive to the signals our children give us and make sure we are present, not only physically, but also emotionally. Creating a secure attachment is a gift we give our children, a gift they will carry with them throughout their lives.

Effective Communication with Children

Effective communication with children is one of the most important pillars for successful and healthy parenting. It is not just about talking to them, but knowing how to listen to them, understand them and convey our messages in a way that truly connects with their emotions and thoughts. The way we communicate with our children not only influences their immediate behavior, but also shapes their self-esteem, their ability to express their emotions and their relationship with us over time. Effective communication not only helps resolve conflicts, but also strengthens the bond between parents and children, creating an environment of trust and mutual respect.

To begin with, it is important to remember that children are not small adults. Although they sometimes seem to understand many things, their way of seeing the world and processing information is different from that of adults. Therefore, when we communicate with them, we must adjust our language and our expectations to their level of development. Speaking to them in a clear, simple and direct manner is key to their understanding. This does not mean that we should treat them as if they do not understand anything, but rather adapt the message to their abilities. Language that is too complicated or abstract can confuse them and cause them to disconnect from the conversation.

Another critical aspect of effective communication is active listening. Often, as parents, we are so focused on teaching and guiding our children that we forget to stop and simply listen to what they have to say. Active listening involves giving them full attention, without interrupting, and showing them that their thoughts and feelings matter. When a child feels heard, they are more likely to open up and share what they are really feeling, which is crucial to building a trusting relationship. Plus, listening doesn't just mean hearing their words, but also paying attention to their body language, facial expressions, and underlying emotions.

It's very common that when a child is feeling frustrated or sad, instead of letting them express what they're feeling, parents immediately try to correct or fix the problem. Even if our intentions are good, this approach can make the child feel like they don't have space to express their emotions or that their feelings aren't important. Instead, it's better to validate what they're feeling. Saying something as simple as "I understand that you feel that way" or "I know that this has upset you" can make a big difference. By validating their emotions, we're teaching them that it's normal to feel frustrated, sad, or angry, and that it's okay to talk about it. This validation is an important step in helping a child learn to manage their own emotions in a healthy way.

In addition to listening and validating, it is essential to be clear and consistent in the messages we send. Sometimes, as parents, we can send mixed messages without realizing it. For example, we may tell them that they should share their toys, but if they then see them being selfish with our own things, the message becomes confusing. Children learn not only from what we tell them, but also from what we do. That is why consistency between our words and our actions is crucial. If we want our children to respect others, we must show respect in our daily lives. If we want them to speak kindly, we must speak kindly to them and to the people around us.

Patience also plays a key role in effective communication. Sometimes, children can be slow to process what we say or express what they are feeling. Instead of rushing them or getting frustrated, it is important to give them the time they need to express themselves. This can be especially important during times of conflict, when emotions are running high. Instead of immediately reacting to misbehavior, it can be helpful to take a moment to breathe and think before responding. Not only does this help us stay calm, but it also teaches our children the importance of reflection before acting.

An important tip is to avoid long lectures or constant criticism. Children, just like adults, do not respond well when they feel attacked or overwhelmed by negative words. Instead of focusing only on what they are doing wrong, it is much more effective to highlight what they are doing well. Praising their efforts and achievements, even if they are small, reinforces positive behaviors and gives them self-confidence. When correction is necessary, it is best to do so constructively, focusing on how they can improve rather than making them feel like they have failed.

Communication doesn't always have to be serious or structured. In fact, many of the best interactions with children happen spontaneously during everyday moments, like while they're playing, eating dinner, or getting ready for bed. These informal moments are perfect opportunities to talk about their days, their friends, or anything that's bothering them. Through these small conversations, we build a strong relationship based on trust and caring. Plus, when children feel comfortable talking to us in the good times, they'll be more willing to come to us in the tough times, too.

One aspect that is often overlooked in communication with children is tone of voice. The tone we use can completely change the meaning of what we say. If we use a harsh or impatient tone, even a positive message can be perceived negatively. In contrast, a calm and loving tone can help soften even the toughest corrections. Children are very sensitive to their parents' tone of voice, and it can influence how they feel about what we are saying to them.

In conclusion, effective communication with children is much more than just talking to them. It is about listening to them attentively, validating their feelings, being consistent in our words and actions, and using an appropriate tone. By doing so, we not only solve problems or correct behaviors, but we also build a relationship of trust and respect that will last a lifetime. Raising children who know how to communicate well and who feel understood begins with us, the parents. By giving them the example and the space to express themselves, we are giving them the necessary tools to face the world with confidence and security.

Positive Discipline

Positive discipline is a way of parenting that seeks to teach children to behave correctly without resorting to harsh or authoritarian punishments. Instead of making children feel afraid or ashamed, positive discipline focuses on helping them understand the consequences of their actions and teaching them to make better decisions in the future. This approach not only promotes respect and cooperation, but also fosters a stronger relationship between parents and children, based on trust and communication.

When we think of discipline, we often associate it with scolding or punishment. However, positive discipline is not about punishing children for doing something wrong, but rather guiding them to learn how to behave appropriately. This involves being firm and consistent, but also kind and understanding. The idea is that children don't just follow the rules because they fear punishment, but because they understand the reason for those rules and the benefits of following them.

A key tenet of positive discipline is the idea of focusing on solutions rather than problems. When a child behaves inappropriately, it's easy to fall into the trap of simply scolding or punishing him or her. However, rather than focusing solely on what the child did wrong, positive discipline invites us to ask ourselves, "What can I do to help him or her learn from this situation?" This might involve talking to the child about what happened, discussing alternatives, and working together to find a solution. In this way, the child not only understands that his or her behavior was inappropriate, but also learns what he or she can do next time to avoid it.

Another important aspect of positive discipline is empathy. This means putting yourself in the child's shoes and trying to understand why they acted the way they did. Many times, children misbehave not because they want to, but because they are frustrated, tired, or don't know how to express what they feel. Instead of reacting angrily, it's helpful to take a moment to breathe and think, "What is my child trying to tell me with this behavior?" By understanding the root of the problem, we can address the situation more effectively and with less conflict.

Positive discipline also focuses on setting clear and consistent boundaries. It helps children to know what is expected of them and what rules they must follow. However, these boundaries should not be rigid or inflexible, but rather tailored to the child's needs and circumstances. It is important to explain to children the reasons behind the rules so that they understand why they are important. When children understand the purpose of the rules, they are more likely to follow them willingly rather than just out of fear of the consequences.

In addition to setting limits, it's important to give children choices and responsibility. This may sound counterintuitive, but when children have some control over their decisions, they are more likely to follow the rules. For example, instead of telling them to "pick up your toys right now," we might offer them choices like, "Would you rather pick up your toys before dinner or after dinner?" This way, the child feels like they have some control over the situation, but in the end, they still have the responsibility to pick up. Giving them the opportunity to make choices also teaches them about the importance of responsibility and the consequences of their choices.

One of the big differences between positive discipline and other, more authoritarian approaches is that positive discipline seeks to reinforce positive behaviors rather than punish negative ones. This means that instead of focusing only on what the child does wrong, we pay more attention to what they do right. Praising and acknowledging a child's efforts, even when they're not perfect, reinforces those behaviors and motivates them to continue acting appropriately. A simple "I love how you picked up your toys without me asking you to" can have a big impact on their attitude.

Still, it's natural for children to make mistakes. Positive discipline doesn't ignore these mistakes, but rather than focusing on punishment, it seeks to teach through natural consequences. Natural consequences are those that occur as a direct result of a child's behavior. For example, if a child refuses to put on a coat when it's cold, the natural consequence is that he will feel cold. These types of consequences help the child understand for himself why certain decisions are not the best ones. In other cases, when natural consequences aren't possible or safe, we can set logical consequences. These should be directly related to the behavior and not punitive. For example, if a child draws on the wall, a logical consequence would be for him to help clean it up.

It's important to remember that positive discipline doesn't mean being permissive or letting children do whatever they want. Instead, it requires firmness and consistency, but always from a place of respect and understanding. Children need clear boundaries and to know that there will be consequences when they don't behave appropriately. However, those consequences shouldn't be seen as punishments, but rather as opportunities to learn and grow.

In the long run, positive discipline has far more profound effects than traditional methods based on punishment. Children who grow up with this approach tend to develop higher self-esteem, as they are taught through respect and understanding rather than fear. They are also often more empathetic, as they have learned to put themselves in the shoes of others and consider the consequences of their actions. Additionally, positive discipline fosters a closer relationship between parent and child, as it is based on open communication and mutual support.

In conclusion, positive discipline is a parenting approach that seeks to teach children how to behave appropriately without resorting to punishment or fear. It is based on empathy, communication, and firmness, and seeks to teach children to make better decisions for themselves. By focusing on solutions and positive behaviors, parents can guide their children in a way that builds their self-esteem and helps them develop important life skills. Positive discipline is not always easy—it requires patience and consistency—but the long-term benefits are immense, for both children and parents.

Setting Boundaries and Standards

Setting boundaries and rules in parenting is one of the most important tasks parents face. Although it can sometimes seem complicated or exhausting, boundaries are essential to children's development. Not only do they help them understand what is expected of them, but they also provide them with a sense of security and structure. Children need to know that there are rules that guide their behavior, and those rules allow them to move through the world more confidently. Contrary to popular belief, boundaries are not something negative or restrictive, but rather a tool that allows them to learn to make decisions and live with others in a respectful and responsible manner.

When we talk about setting boundaries, it is important to understand that it is not about imposing a set of strict rules without explanation, but about creating an environment in which children can explore, make mistakes and learn, but always within certain margins that ensure their well-being. Clear and consistent boundaries are like a guide that helps them know what is right and what is not. They teach them that every action has a consequence, and this is crucial for their emotional and social development.

One of the first things parents need to keep in mind when setting limits is that they should be appropriate for the child's age. We cannot expect the same level of self-control or understanding from a three-year-old as from a ten-year-old. As children grow, their abilities to understand and follow rules also evolve. Therefore, limits need to be flexible and adapt to the child's development. For example, while a toddler may be taught not to touch the stove because it is dangerous, an older child may understand the reason behind the rule and be more aware of the risks. It is essential that limits are understandable and reasonable for each stage of development.

It's also important to be consistent. Children need to know that rules apply all the time, not just when it's convenient for parents. If you allow something one day and then forbid it the next without a clear reason, your child will become confused and have a hard time understanding what is really expected of him. This inconsistency can lead to frustration, as the child doesn't know when he's doing the right thing. That's why it's important for parents to be firm and consistent in enforcing rules, so that children understand that the rules are always the same and that they are applied fairly.

Sometimes children may test boundaries to see how far they can go. This is completely normal and part of their learning. In fact, when children push boundaries, they are not necessarily challenging our authority; rather, they are exploring the world and trying to understand how relationships and rules work in their environment. As parents, it is essential to not lose our cool in these situations and to remember that our job is to guide them patiently and firmly. Giving in to bad behavior or changing the rules on the spot can send the wrong message. Instead, we need to maintain boundaries and explain why they are important.

Another key aspect of setting rules is clarity. Children, especially younger ones, need rules to be specific and easy to understand. Instead of giving them vague instructions like "behave," it's better to be more specific, saying something like "I want you to use a calm voice while we're in the library." This way, children know exactly what is expected of them in specific situations. Clear, direct rules make it easier for children to follow, as there is no confusion about what they should do.

However, it is not enough to simply set limits and expect children to simply follow them. It is important to explain to them why these rules exist. When children understand the reason behind a rule, they are more likely to respect it and follow it on their own initiative. For example, instead of simply forbidding a child to watch television before doing homework, we can explain to them that it is important to finish responsibilities first so that they can then have free time without worries. In this way, children begin to see rules not as arbitrary impositions, but as tools that help them organize their lives more effectively.

Many times when children break a rule, it's easy to fall back on immediate punishment as a solution. However, it's more beneficial to use these moments as opportunities to teach. Instead of simply saying "you can't do that," we can help them reflect on their behavior and the consequences of their actions. For example, if a child breaks the rule of sharing their toys with their friends, we can talk to them about how they would feel if they were the one who didn't get any. These types of discussions help them develop empathy and understand the impact of their actions on others.

Another approach that can be helpful is to allow children to participate in creating the rules. When children feel that they have a say in the decisions that affect their daily lives, they are more likely to follow the rules more willingly. Of course, this doesn't mean that parents should give up their authority, but by involving children in the process of setting certain rules, we give them the opportunity to feel that their opinions matter. For example, we might ask them, "What do you think would be a good time to go to bed?" or "How do you think we can organize time so that you can play after doing your homework?" This way, children feel like they are part of the process and better understand why certain rules are set.

When correcting behavior, it is important to use logical consequences rather than punishments that are not related to the action. For example, if a child breaks a toy because he or she was using it inappropriately, a logical consequence would be that he or she cannot play with that toy for a while or that he or she must help repair it if possible. This helps the child understand the relationship between his or her behavior and its consequences, and teaches him or her to be more responsible.

It's important to remember that boundaries aren't designed to restrict children's freedom, but rather to teach them to make responsible decisions and to respect others. Clear, consistent boundaries provide a structure within which children can explore, learn, and grow. Children who grow up with well-established boundaries are more likely to develop self-control skills, make responsible decisions, and follow rules both at home and in other settings, such as school or the community.

Setting boundaries and rules also has a positive impact on the parent-child relationship. When parents are consistent and clear in their expectations, children feel more secure and confident. They know what is expected of them and understand that parents are there to guide and support them. This trusting relationship strengthens over time, making communication and conflict resolution easier as children grow.

In short, setting boundaries and rules is essential to guiding children in their development. These boundaries, when clear, consistent, and age-appropriate, not only teach children to behave responsibly, but also provide a sense of security and structure. Involving children in the process, explaining the reasons behind the rules, and using logical consequences rather than punishment are all approaches that foster learning and growth. Although it can be challenging, setting effective boundaries is a long-term investment in children's emotional and social well-being.

Motivation and Reinforcement in Parenting

Motivation and reinforcement are essential tools in parenting. Through them, parents can influence their children's behavior in positive ways, helping them learn, grow, and develop. All children need to feel motivated to learn new skills, meet their parents' expectations, and generally behave appropriately. However, it can often be difficult to know how to effectively motivate them or what type of reinforcements to use to encourage good behavior.

To better understand how motivation and reinforcement work in parenting, it's important to keep in mind that children, like anyone, respond best when they feel supported, valued, and rewarded for their efforts. Often, children not only need to know what to do, but they also need a reason to do it. This is where motivation comes in. Motivation can come from many sources, but in parenting, much of it comes from children's desire to please their parents, feel successful, or receive some sort of reward, whether emotional or material.

Intrinsic motivation is motivation that comes from within. It is when a child feels driven to do something because he or she enjoys it or finds satisfaction in doing it. For example, a child who loves to draw can spend hours concentrating on creating his or her own drawings, without needing anyone to tell him or her to do so. This type of motivation is very powerful, and as parents, it is important to encourage these natural interests. If a child is intrinsically motivated to learn something, such as reading or playing a sport, parents can support them by offering opportunities for them to do so and encouraging them to keep going when they encounter difficulties.

However, not all desirable behaviors come with intrinsic motivation. There are many tasks and responsibilities that children may not find particularly engaging or interesting, such as doing homework or helping with chores. This is where extrinsic motivation plays an important role. Extrinsic motivation comes from external rewards, such as praise, material rewards, or privileges. While extrinsic motivation is not always as long-lasting as intrinsic motivation, it can be a great way to jumpstart positive behavior until the child begins to find satisfaction in the task on its own.

One of the most effective ways to use extrinsic motivation in parenting is through positive reinforcement. Positive reinforcement involves rewarding children when they display the behavior you want. These rewards don't have to be material or large. In fact, something as simple as sincere praise can be a very powerful reinforcer. When children receive positive attention for their efforts, they feel valued and motivated to continue behaving in that way. For example, if a child finishes his or her homework on time, a comment like, "Wow, that was great! I'm proud of you for finishing before dinner" can be enough to reinforce that behavior.

Positive reinforcement works best when it is immediate and directly related to the behavior. If a child behaves well at the grocery store, rather than waiting to praise him later, it is much more effective to do so in the moment: "I love how you waited patiently while we shopped." This helps the child connect the behavior with the reward. Also, reinforcements should be consistent at first, so that the child clearly understands which behaviors are being reinforced. As the child internalizes those behaviors, reinforcements can be given less frequently as the child begins to behave appropriately without expecting a constant reward.

However, it's important not to confuse positive reinforcement with bribery. A bribe is when parents promise a reward before the child has shown the appropriate behavior, while positive reinforcement is offered after the desired behavior has already occurred. For example, if a parent says, "I'll give you a treat if you stop making noise," they're offering a bribe. On the other hand, if the child has already been quiet and the parent then praises or rewards the child, they're using positive reinforcement. Bribery can teach the child to misbehave on purpose in order to get a reward, while positive reinforcement reinforces good behavior that has already occurred.

In addition to positive reinforcement, parents can also use negative reinforcement to motivate appropriate behavior. Despite its name, negative reinforcement does not involve punishment or negative consequences, but rather the removal of something the child finds unpleasant when he or she displays the appropriate behavior. For example, if a child complains about having to do his or her homework, a negative reinforcement might be that he or she is allowed to stop doing it once he or she has completed a certain amount of work well done. In this way, the child learns that by doing his or her homework efficiently, he or she can be spared an unpleasant experience.

It's crucial that reinforcements are appropriate for the child's age and the situation. Young children, for example, respond well to verbal praise and small, tangible rewards, such as stickers or extra play time. As children get older, they may be more motivated by recognition of their accomplishments or by receiving additional privileges, such as more time with their friends or increased autonomy in their daily decisions. The key is to know your child and what really motivates them, as what works for one child may not work for another.

Of course, not all desirable behavior can be reinforced or motivated by external rewards. In the long term, the goal is for children to develop an internal motivation to act appropriately. To foster this internal motivation, parents should help children understand why certain behaviors are important. For example, if a child helps set the table, we should not only praise his action, but also explain to him why his contribution is valuable to the family: "Thank you for helping with the table, that makes the work go faster and we can all eat dinner together." By doing this, we help children see the intrinsic value in their actions and find motivation in the well-being of others, not just in rewards.

Throughout the parenting process, it's important to remember that motivation doesn't always have to come in the form of big rewards or exaggerated praise. Sometimes, simply paying attention to a child's efforts and acknowledging them is enough to motivate them. Children seek approval and affection from their parents, and often, that validation can be one of the most powerful forms of motivation. Showing genuine interest in what they do, talking with them about their accomplishments, and sharing moments of celebration for their efforts can have a profound impact on their desire to keep going and improve.

It's also important to be patient. Sometimes the results of our efforts to motivate and reinforce appropriate behavior aren't immediately apparent. We may have to repeat praise or reinforce certain behaviors several times before the child adopts them naturally. However, over time, positive reinforcement and proper motivation help build habits that will last a lifetime.

In summary, motivation and reinforcement are powerful tools in parenting that help children learn and develop positive behaviors. Both intrinsic and extrinsic motivation have their place in the learning process, and positive reinforcements are a great way to reinforce good behavior. As children grow, it is important for parents to guide them toward greater internal motivation, teaching them to find satisfaction and value in their actions, beyond external rewards. Through patience, consistency, and love, parents can help their children develop into motivated, responsible, and empathetic individuals.

Alexa Murphy

Managing Tantrums

Tantrums are a common and natural part of child development. Parents often feel frustrated or overwhelmed when their children have one, especially if it happens in public or at inconvenient times. However, it's important to remember that tantrums are not a sign of bad behavior or poor parenting. In fact, they are a way for children, especially younger ones, to express their emotions when they don't know how to handle them otherwise. Learning to handle these situations with patience and understanding can make a big difference in parenting.

To better understand why children throw tantrums, it's important to remember that at a young age, they haven't yet fully developed the ability to regulate their emotions. Something that might seem insignificant to an adult, like not being able to eat a sweet or having to put on a coat, can feel like a catastrophe to a young child. At these times, a child is feeling overwhelmed by frustration, tiredness, or overstimulation, and a tantrum is their way of releasing all those pent-up emotions. It's not something a child does intentionally to manipulate parents, but rather a reaction to feeling out of control.

One of the first steps to managing tantrums effectively is to try to prevent them before they happen. While it's not always possible to avoid tantrums, there are certain factors that tend to trigger them, and parents can take steps to minimize them. For example, many children have more tantrums when they are tired, hungry, or overstimulated. Making sure children are well-rested, have eaten on time, and have calm moments can reduce the chances of an emotional outburst. It's also helpful to anticipate situations that tend to cause frustration. If you know your child has trouble leaving the park, you can warn them ahead of time, "We're leaving in five minutes," or "After this game, we're going home." This helps them mentally prepare for the change and feel more in control.

When a tantrum occurs, the most important thing is to stay calm. It's natural for parents to feel irritated or stressed when their child is screaming or crying, especially if other people are present. However, responding with anger or despair will only escalate the situation. Children, especially younger ones, are very sensitive to their parents' emotions, and if they sense that their parents are losing control, too, the tantrum is likely to get worse. Instead, it's helpful to take a deep breath, keep a calm tone of voice, and try to empathize with what the child is feeling, even if you can't give in to their demand.

Showing empathy doesn't mean giving in to a child's every demand, but rather acknowledging their emotions. You can say something like, "I know you're really upset because you wanted that toy, but now is not the time." These types of statements help a child feel understood and validated, which can often calm the intensity of the tantrum. It's also important to remember that in the midst of a tantrum, children are not in a state of mind where they can reason or negotiate. Trying to explain to them why their behavior is inappropriate or why they can't have what they want probably won't work until they've calmed down.

A helpful strategy during tantrums is to offer the child a safe space to vent his emotions. This may mean taking him to a quieter place where he can be away from distractions or stimuli that may aggravate his frustration. Some children respond well to a physical space, such as their room, where they can calm down without feeling watched or pressured. Other children prefer to have their parents nearby during a tantrum, even if they are not ready to talk or be comforted right away. Every child is different, and parents should be sensitive to their child's individual needs at these times.

It's important not to unintentionally reinforce tantrums. Sometimes parents, in their desperation for a tantrum to end, may give in to a child's demands, giving them what they wanted to calm them down. However, this can teach a child that tantrums are an effective way to get what they want. If a child learns that screaming or crying gets them that toy or candy they were initially denied, they're likely to resort to the same strategy in the future. That's why it's essential to stand firm once a limit has been set, without giving in to a child's demands in the middle of a tantrum.

As your child calms down, it's a good time to offer comfort and support. This isn't about punishing or scolding your child for his tantrum, but about helping him process what happened. Once you're both calm, you can talk about what happened: "You seemed really upset because you couldn't have that toy. Would you like to tell me more about how you felt?" This type of conversation not only validates your child's feelings, but it also gives him a chance to start putting words to his emotions. Over time, this type of reflection can help your child learn to express his feelings more effectively instead of resorting to a tantrum.

Another effective strategy is to teach children coping skills, so they can better handle their emotions next time. For example, you can teach deep breathing techniques, such as inhaling slowly through the nose and exhaling through the mouth, or how to count to ten when feeling frustrated. These little tricks can be powerful tools for a child to learn how to calm themselves down. Additionally, parents can model how to handle stress or frustration in a calm manner, as children learn a lot by watching how their parents respond to their own emotions.

It's important to note that tantrums don't last forever. They're most common during the two- to five-year age group, when children are still learning to regulate their emotions and communicate effectively. Over time, as they develop language skills and strategies for dealing with frustration, tantrums tend to lessen. However, how parents handle tantrums during this stage can greatly influence how children learn to manage their emotions in the future.

Alexa Murphy

Fostering Self-Esteem and Confidence in Children

Building self-esteem and confidence in children is one of the most important aspects of parenting, as these are the pillars on which children will build their identity and their way of interacting with the world. A child with healthy self-esteem and well-developed confidence not only feels capable of facing challenges, but is also more resilient, recovers better from difficulties, and has a more positive view of themselves and their capabilities. However, building self-esteem and confidence is not something that happens overnight, but is an ongoing process that requires time, patience, and dedication.

Self-esteem is, in essence, children's perception of themselves. It's how they value themselves, what they believe they are capable of doing, and how they feel about who they are as a person. Children are not born with a defined self-esteem; it is developed through the experiences they have and interactions with the people around them, especially their parents. That's why it's so important for parents to play an active role in helping their children build a positive self-image.

One of the most effective ways to foster self-esteem in children is through unconditional love and acceptance. Children need to know that they are loved and valued, not just for what they do, but for who they are. This means that even when they make mistakes or misbehave, they need to feel that their parents' love is not at stake. By providing a safe and caring environment, parents send the message that children are worthy of love, regardless of their successes or failures. This sense of being loved unconditionally is the foundation upon which strong self-esteem is built.

It's crucial for parents to provide praise appropriately. While praise is a powerful tool for building self-esteem, it's important that it's genuine and specific. Praising a child for being "smart" or "good" may seem positive, but in reality, it can make a child feel like their worth is tied to those things. Instead, it's better to praise concrete efforts and accomplishments: "I love how hard you put into that drawing, you really put in a lot of work," or "I'm proud of how you tried to solve that math problem." By doing this, parents reinforce the idea that it's not about being perfect, but about effort and perseverance.

Another key aspect of building self-esteem is allowing children to make choices and take on age-appropriate challenges. When children are given the opportunity to make decisions, whether it's something as simple as choosing their clothes or deciding what activity they want to do, they are taught that their opinions and desires are valuable. This also helps them develop a sense of control over their lives, which increases their self-confidence. Of course, the decisions they are allowed to make should be appropriate for their level of maturity, but even small choices can have a big impact on their sense of autonomy.

Additionally, it's important for parents to allow children to experience failure and difficulty. While it's natural to want to protect children from disappointment, preventing them from facing challenges can prevent them from developing confidence in their abilities to overcome obstacles. Children who never experience failure may come to doubt their abilities or become afraid to try again. Instead, when a child fails or faces a difficulty, parents should support their effort, acknowledge their frustration, and encourage them to keep going. "I know it was hard not to win that game, but I'm impressed that you kept trying until the end. What do you think you could do differently next time?" This approach not only builds self-esteem, but it also teaches children the importance of resilience.

Another way to build self-esteem is by helping children develop a positive self-image through constructive feedback. All children, just like adults, will make mistakes and mess up at some point. Instead of criticizing or making the child feel bad about those mistakes, it's more helpful to focus on how they can learn from the situation. For example, if a child doesn't complete a task on time, instead of saying, "You're always late, you never do anything right," parents can say, "It seems like it was hard to finish on time this time. How do you think you could be better organized next time?" This type of feedback helps the child see mistakes as opportunities to improve rather than feeling like they've failed hopelessly.

Modeling also plays a crucial role in developing self-esteem and confidence. Children constantly watch their parents and the adults around them, and their behaviors and attitudes have a huge impact on how children view the world and themselves. If parents model a positive attitude toward themselves, accept their own mistakes, and show confidence in their abilities, children will learn to do the same. On the other hand, if parents are critical of themselves or show low self-esteem, children may internalize those behaviors. It is important for parents to model how to handle difficulties with confidence and optimism.

Activities that foster a sense of accomplishment are also essential to building children's self-esteem. Participating in activities that allow them to develop new skills, such as sports, music, art, or any other area of interest, can make children feel capable and proud of their accomplishments. Parents can support these efforts by providing praise for effort and dedication, not just the end result. For example, if a child has been practicing a musical instrument, it's important to acknowledge their progress and effort: "I can hear how much you've improved on that song, it's getting better and better." These types of comments reinforce the idea that progress is just as valuable as the end result.

It's also important to teach children to be kind to themselves. Children, like adults, can be very hard on themselves when they feel like they've failed or when things don't go their way. Teaching them to use positive self-talk and to be compassionate about their own mistakes can have a big impact on their self-esteem. Parents can model this verbally: "Sometimes I make mistakes, but the important thing is that I keep learning and trying again." By learning to treat themselves with kindness and understanding, children develop stronger self-esteem that is less dependent on outside approval.

It's crucial to remember that self-esteem is not the same as selfishness or arrogance. Fostering healthy self-esteem in children doesn't mean making them feel better than others, but rather helping them feel confident and comfortable in their own skin. A child with healthy self-esteem doesn't need to compare themselves to others or constantly seek external validation. Instead, they feel capable, valuable, and confident in who they are, without needing to put others down to feel good.

Finally, the role of parents in developing their children's self-esteem is ongoing and evolves over time. As children grow, their challenges change, and so do the ways in which they need support and validation. However, the core principles remain the same: unconditional love, genuine praise, opportunities to make choices and face challenges, and positive modeling. When parents cultivate these aspects in parenting, they help their children develop strong self-esteem and confidence that will serve them for life.

Self-esteem and confidence are essential for children to become confident adults, capable of facing the challenges that life throws at them. With the right support, children can learn to value themselves, believe in their abilities and grow into confident and empathetic individuals, ready to face the world with optimism and determination.

The Importance of Play in Development

Play is one of the most important activities in a child's life. Although to adults it may seem like just a way to entertain themselves or pass the time, in reality, play is fundamental to children's physical, emotional, social and cognitive development. Through play, children learn about the world around them, develop essential skills and begin to understand their own and others' emotions. It is a powerful tool that fosters their growth in multiple aspects, and it is crucial that parents understand its importance in order to support and encourage it in the best possible way.

Play is not just about fun, it's also about learning. Children learn by doing, and play allows them to explore, experiment and discover freely and safely. From the moment a baby grabs a rattle or a child builds a tower of blocks, they are developing important skills without even realising it. In this sense, play gives them the opportunity to develop their motor skills, whether by running, jumping, manipulating small objects or using play tools. Each action they perform helps them to better coordinate their movements and strengthen their body.

Cognitive development is also supported by play. When children play, they are constantly facing challenges and solving problems. When building a tower of blocks, for example, they have to think about how to make it higher or how to stop it from falling over. If they are playing with puzzles, they must use their logic and reasoning skills to fit the pieces into the right places. These types of activities not only develop their problem-solving abilities, but also encourage their creativity and critical thinking. In symbolic play, where children pretend to be other people or animals, they use their imagination to create complex stories and situations, which helps them to better understand the world around them and develop their ability to think abstractly.

Play is also crucial for emotional development. Through different forms of play, children learn to recognize and manage their own emotions. A child playing at being a superhero may be exploring their feelings of power and control, while another playing with dolls may be processing their feelings of caring and empathy. Play allows children to safely express their emotions, which helps them understand them better and learn how to manage them in real-life situations. Additionally, when they play with other children, they are forced to confront a variety of emotions, such as frustration when they lose a game, joy when they achieve a goal, or patience when they must wait their turn. Through these experiences, children learn to regulate their emotions and develop greater emotional intelligence.

In social terms, play is one of the first opportunities children have to interact with others in a structured way. As they grow older, they begin to engage in cooperative play, where they must work together to achieve a common goal, such as in team games or shared construction activities. In these situations, children learn important social skills, such as communication, negotiation, conflict resolution, and cooperation. They learn to listen to others, compromise, and share, which is critical to their social development and ability to form healthy relationships later in life. Play is one of the first ways children experience teamwork and respect for rules and turn-taking.

In addition to social play, it is also important to recognize the value of individual play. When children play alone, they have the opportunity to explore their own interests and develop their independence. This type of play is equally valuable, as it allows children to discover what they like and dislike, and in turn, strengthens their ability to focus on a task and stay engaged without the need for the constant presence of an adult or other children. Individual play also encourages self-reflection, as children are free to create and explore at their own pace, without the influence or expectations of others.

Outdoor play, in particular, has multiple additional benefits. It allows children to connect with nature, explore their physical surroundings, and develop a greater appreciation for the natural world. Running, climbing, jumping, and exploring outdoors not only supports physical development, but also provides children with the opportunity to experience controlled risk. Climbing a tree, running up a hill, or building a fort out of branches teaches children to assess situations, measure their own boundaries, and make decisions about what is safe and unsafe. These types of experiences contribute to increasing their self-confidence and developing a sense of accomplishment.

It is also important to note that play does not always have to be structured or directed by adults. Sometimes parents fall into the trap of wanting to direct their children's play or constantly planning activities. While organized activities have their place and are valuable, it is also crucial to allow children to play freely and spontaneously. Unstructured play, where children have full control over what they want to do, allows them to develop their creativity, problem-solving skills, and independence. This type of play also teaches children self-management and responsibility for their own decisions, as they are the ones who decide the rules, stories, and goals of the game.

Play can also be a valuable tool for strengthening the bond between parents and children. When parents engage in their children's play, they are sending the message that they value the time they spend together and that they are interested in what their children enjoy. Playing with their children not only strengthens the relationship, but it also gives parents the opportunity to observe and learn more about their children's personalities, interests, and way of seeing the world. This shared play time can be as simple as building something with blocks, playing a board game, or making up a story together. It's not the activity itself that's important, but the quality time and connection that is established during play.

In short, play is much more than just a form of entertainment for children. It is an essential tool for their development in all areas: physical, cognitive, emotional and social. Through play, children explore, learn, develop and prepare to face the world. Parents play a fundamental role in supporting and encouraging this process, whether by providing them with time and space to play, getting involved in their play or simply allowing them the freedom to explore and create at their own pace. By understanding the importance of play and its role in child development, parents can help their children grow up in a healthy, happy and balanced way.

Emotional Intelligence in Children

Emotional intelligence is one of the most important skills children can develop from an early age. Unlike IQ, which measures skills such as logic and problem-solving, emotional intelligence refers to the ability to understand and manage emotions, both one's own and those of others. In daily life, emotional intelligence plays a crucial role in relationships, in the way people face challenges, and in the way difficult situations are handled. In children, developing this skill helps them to be more empathetic, to understand their own feelings, and to interact in healthier ways with others.

From a very young age, children experience a wide range of emotions. They may feel joy when they are playing with a friend, sadness when they lose a favorite toy, or frustration when they fail at something they try. However, they often don't have the tools to identify and manage these feelings. This is where emotional intelligence comes into play. Teaching children to recognize what they are feeling and to name those emotions is the first step in developing their emotional intelligence. For example, if a child is upset because he or she couldn't win a game, it's important for parents to help them identify that feeling: "It sounds like you're frustrated because things didn't go the way you wanted. It's okay to feel that way." This simple act of putting into words what a child is feeling not only validates their emotions, but it also teaches them to recognize them.

Emotional intelligence also involves learning how to manage emotions appropriately. Children, like adults, can sometimes feel overwhelmed by their feelings. A young child who is frustrated may start crying or have a tantrum because they don't yet know how to channel their frustration in another way. This is where parents can step in to teach emotional regulation strategies. Instead of ignoring or minimizing a child's emotions, parents can offer them tools to manage what they are feeling. For example, if a child is feeling very angry, parents can teach them to take deep breaths to calm down or to step away from the situation for a moment until they feel calmer. These are skills that children can learn and practice over time, and that will be useful throughout their lives.

A key aspect of emotional intelligence is empathy, which is the ability to understand and share the feelings of others. Developing empathy in children not only helps them build healthier relationships, but also fosters an environment of respect and understanding. Children who learn to be empathetic are better able to put themselves in the shoes of others and respond more appropriately to the emotional needs of the people around them. A simple example of how empathy can be fostered in children is by helping them reflect on how others feel in certain situations. If a child takes a toy from his brother, parents can ask, "How do you think your brother feels when you take his toy away? What could you do to make him feel better?" These questions not only help the child think about the emotions of others, but also guide him toward making more empathetic decisions.

Another important aspect of emotional intelligence is self-awareness. This skill allows children to be more aware of their own emotions and how they affect their behavior. When children are able to identify their feelings, they can make more informed decisions about how to act. For example, if a child is aware that they are starting to feel frustrated, they may decide to take a break before their emotions lead to impulsive behavior, such as yelling or pushing another child. Parents can help develop this self-awareness by encouraging their children to talk about what they are feeling and how certain emotions affect their decisions. A simple "How are you feeling right now?" can be a great way to start a conversation that helps a child reflect on their emotions.

Emotional intelligence is also linked to children's ability to handle interpersonal relationships in a healthy manner. Children who have higher emotional intelligence are better able to resolve conflicts effectively, as they can see things from others' points of view and manage their own emotions during tense situations. For example, if two children are arguing about who should be the leader in a game, those who have developed their emotional intelligence may be more willing to listen to others' perspectives and come to an agreement, rather than simply insisting on getting their way. Teaching children to resolve conflicts peacefully is an essential part of developing emotional intelligence. Parents can model these skills at home by showing how disagreements are resolved respectfully and without resorting to yelling or punishment.

In addition to all of this, it is important for children to learn to be resilient – how to manage difficult emotions and bounce back from stressful situations. Resilience is an important part of emotional intelligence, as it enables children to face life's challenges with a more positive attitude and the ability to bounce back from adversity. Resilient children are better able to deal with failure or disappointment without losing self-confidence or feeling overwhelmed by their emotions. Parents can foster resilience by helping children see problems as learning opportunities rather than failures. If a child fails to achieve something they tried, instead of saying, "Don't worry, it wasn't that big of a deal," parents can say, "It's normal to feel disappointed, but think about what you could do differently next time." This type of approach helps children learn that difficulties are not insurmountable and that they can find solutions to problems.

Emotional intelligence isn't something that children develop on their own; it requires support and guidance from the adults in their lives. Parents play a crucial role in modeling emotionally intelligent behavior. Children constantly observe how their parents handle emotions and social interactions. If parents react calmly and understandingly to difficult situations, children will learn to do the same. On the other hand, if parents tend to react with anger or frustration, children are likely to imitate that behavior. That's why it's so important for parents to work on their own emotional intelligence and show their children how to handle emotions in healthy ways.

It's important to keep in mind that every child is different, and some may develop emotional intelligence faster than others. Some children are naturally more sensitive to the emotions of others, while others may need more time and support to learn how to recognize and manage their emotions. In any case, it's essential for parents to be patient and provide an environment where children feel safe to express their feelings. Creating a space where emotions are validated and not judged allows children to feel more comfortable sharing what they're feeling and learning to manage their emotions more effectively.

In conclusion, emotional intelligence is an essential skill that helps children develop healthy relationships, manage their emotions, and deal with life's challenges more effectively. Parents play a key role in this process, providing support, guidance, and role modeling. By teaching children to identify, understand, and manage their emotions, as well as to be empathetic toward others, parents are helping to prepare their children for a more balanced, happy, and fulfilling life. Through patience, emotional support, and example, parents can significantly contribute to the development of their children's emotional intelligence, something that will benefit them not only in childhood, but throughout their entire lives.

How to Treat Childhood Anxiety and Stress

Anxiety and stress are not emotions that are exclusive to adults; children can also experience these feelings at different times in their lives. However, unlike adults, children often do not have the tools to understand what they are feeling or to manage those feelings appropriately. Anxiety and stress in children can arise for a variety of reasons, from changes in their environment, such as starting a new school or facing an unfamiliar situation, to family or social issues. The important thing is that, as parents, we can identify these moments of anxiety and stress, and offer children the support they need to overcome them in a healthy way.

One of the first signs that a child is experiencing anxiety or stress is a change in their behavior. You might notice that they are more irritable than usual, have trouble sleeping, or are more withdrawn in social situations. Some children may manifest their anxiety through physical complaints, such as headaches or stomachaches, as sometimes their emotional stress is reflected in their body. It's also common for anxious children to avoid certain situations or activities that they once enjoyed, as they may feel overwhelmed by fear or worry. If you see any of these behaviors in your child, it's important to approach them with empathy and understanding, rather than dismissing them as temporary or unimportant.

Once you've identified that your child may be dealing with anxiety or stress, it's crucial to create a safe space where they can talk about what they're feeling. Often, children don't have the emotional vocabulary to clearly express what's going on for them, so it's helpful for parents to ask open-ended questions that invite the child to talk. Instead of asking, "Why are you stressed?" you could say something like, "I've noticed that you've been a little worried lately. Is there something bothering you?" These types of questions give children the opportunity to share their worries without feeling pressured or judged. It's important that when they do talk, you listen carefully and validate their feelings. Saying something as simple as, "It's normal to feel worried sometimes" can make children feel understood and supported.

One of the most effective ways to help children manage anxiety and stress is to teach them relaxation techniques. These techniques not only help them calm down in the moment, but they also give them tools they can use in the future when faced with stressful situations. One of the simplest and most effective techniques is deep breathing. When children feel anxious, their breathing tends to be rapid and shallow, which can intensify feelings of stress. Teaching them to breathe slowly and deeply can help reduce those feelings of anxiety. You can have them practice this with you, asking them to imagine that they are blowing up a large balloon and that they must fill the balloon with their slow, steady breathing. This exercise teaches them to take control of their breathing and therefore feel calmer.

Another technique that can be helpful is the use of visualizations. You can invite your child to close their eyes and imagine themselves in a place that makes them feel safe and calm, such as a beach or a park. Ask them to imagine the details of that place: the sound of the waves, the warmth of the sun, or the birdsong. By focusing on this relaxing image, your child can divert their attention from what is causing them stress and feel calmer. These visualizations can be very helpful before situations that cause anxiety, such as going to school or facing something that worries them.

In addition to relaxation techniques, it's important to help children understand that stress and anxiety are normal emotions that we all experience at some point. It's not about eliminating these emotions altogether, as they are a part of life, but rather about learning how to manage them in a healthy way. Children need to understand that it's okay to feel nervous or worried from time to time, but it's also important for them to know that they have the power to control how they react to those feelings. Parents can help convey this message by sharing their own experiences with stress and anxiety, showing them that even adults deal with these feelings, but that there are ways to cope.

Physical activity is also a powerful tool for reducing anxiety and stress in children. Not only is exercise beneficial for physical health, but it also has a positive impact on emotional well-being. When children are active, their bodies release endorphins, which are mood-boosting and stress-reducing chemicals. Plus, exercise offers them a way to release pent-up energy that may be contributing to their anxiety. Children don't need to participate in organized sports activities to reap these benefits. Something as simple as going for a walk, run, or playing in the park can be enough to help them release tension and feel better.

Free play can also be a great way to help children relax and forget about their worries for a while. Through play, children can creatively express their emotions and release any tension they may be feeling. Role-playing, for example, where children pretend to be another person or situation, can help them process their feelings in a safe and controlled way. If a child is stressed about a test at school, they may want to play the role of teacher or student, allowing them to explore their emotions in a judgment-free environment.

It's also important to establish a daily routine that provides structure and predictability for children. Stress can often arise from uncertainty and a lack of control over situations. Having a clear and predictable routine can help children feel more secure and less anxious. This doesn't mean that every moment of the day needs to be planned, but it does mean that there are certain consistent elements, such as regular times for eating, playing, and sleeping. Knowing what's going to happen next can provide children with a sense of stability in the midst of any stressful situation.

It's also critical that children have enough time to relax. Often, children's schedules are packed with activities, which can increase their stress. While it's important for them to participate in activities they enjoy, they also need time to simply be kids, without the pressure of meeting commitments or expectations. Make sure your child has time to relax and unwind, without scheduled activities, which will allow them to recharge and reduce stress.

Finally, in some cases, children's anxiety or stress may be deeper and more persistent, and they may need additional support. If you notice that your child is dealing with anxiety or stress on a consistent basis and that their emotions are interfering with their ability to enjoy daily life, it might be helpful to seek help from a professional. A child psychologist can work with the child to teach them more advanced stress and anxiety management techniques, as well as help identify any underlying causes that may be contributing to their feelings.

In short, anxiety and stress are common emotions in children, but with the right support, they can learn to manage them in a healthy way. Parents play a crucial role by providing a supportive environment, actively listening to their children, teaching them relaxation techniques, and modeling healthy ways to manage stress. By helping children understand and manage their anxiety, you are not only providing them with relief in the moment, but you are also equipping them with valuable skills that will serve them throughout their lives.

The Influence of the Family Environment on Child Behavior

The family environment is one of the most important factors in a child's development and behaviour. From the moment they are born, children absorb everything they see, hear and feel in their home. It is in this environment that they begin to form their first ideas about the world, about how to interact with others and about themselves. Therefore, it is crucial to understand how family dynamics can influence children's behaviour, in order to provide them with an environment that fosters their emotional and social growth in a positive way.

Children are like little sponges that absorb everything that happens around them. From a very young age, they observe how their parents and other family members behave, and they tend to imitate what they see. If a child grows up in an environment where patience, mutual respect and effective communication prevail, he or she is likely to adopt those same values and reflect them in his or her behavior. On the contrary, if the child is exposed to shouting, constant fights or lack of communication, it is also likely that these attitudes will be reflected in his or her way of acting.

One of the clearest ways in which the family environment influences children's behavior is through the way parents handle their emotions and conflicts. Children watch closely how their parents respond to stress, frustration, or everyday problems, and often reproduce those responses. If parents are able to manage their emotions in a calm and controlled manner, and resolve conflicts with respect and empathy, children will learn that this is an effective and healthy way to deal with difficulties. However, if parents respond to challenges with yelling, insults, or violence, children may adopt those same behaviors as defense mechanisms or forms of communication.

Another important aspect is consistency in parenting. Children need a stable and predictable environment to feel safe and confident. When rules and expectations are clear and consistent, children know what is expected of them and what the boundaries are. This helps them develop a sense of responsibility and understand the consequences of their actions. On the other hand, if rules at home are constantly changing or not consistently enforced, children may feel confused and frustrated, which can lead to defiant or inappropriate behavior. Consistency refers not only to rules, but also to the affection and attention that parents provide. A home where children receive constant love, support, and understanding supports their emotional well-being and reinforces positive behaviors.

The parenting style adopted by parents also plays a fundamental role in the behavior of their children. There are different parenting styles, and each has a different impact on the development of children. The authoritarian style, for example, is characterized by being strict and inflexible, where parents impose rules with no room for dialogue. Children who grow up in this type of environment may develop rebellious behavior or, on the contrary, become very submissive, as they are not allowed to express their opinions or emotions freely. In contrast, the permissive style is based on almost total freedom, with few clear rules or boundaries. Children raised under this approach may develop impulsive or defiant behavior, as they do not learn to regulate their actions or respect limits.

The democratic style, on the other hand, is presented as a more balanced option, where parents establish clear rules, but also encourage dialogue and mutual understanding. In this type of environment, children learn to make decisions, take responsibility for their actions, and express their feelings in a healthy way. This parenting style tends to generate more positive behaviors, as children feel valued and respected, while understanding the importance of following rules and limits.

The quality of relationships between family members also has a direct impact on children's behavior. A home where caring and supportive relationships prevail creates an environment in which children feel safe and loved. In this type of environment, children typically develop stronger self-esteem, which is reflected in more assertive and less dependent behaviors. However, when family relationships are marked by tension, conflict, or indifference, children may feel insecure or emotionally abandoned, which can lead to aggressive, defiant, or withdrawn behaviors.

It is important to note that it is not only the relationship between parents and children that influences children's behavior, but also the relationship between the parents. Children observe how their parents interact with each other, and often those interactions serve as a model for their own relationships in the future. If parents treat each other with respect and consideration, children are likely to internalize those same values. In contrast, if parents are in constant conflict or show disinterest in each other, children may experience feelings of anxiety or insecurity, which can manifest in problematic behaviors.

Another crucial aspect is how parents handle their children's mistakes or difficulties. A family environment where children are allowed to make mistakes without being punished harshly fosters learning and growth. When parents respond to mistakes with patience and teach children to learn from their mistakes, they are given the opportunity to develop problem-solving skills and resilience. Conversely, if mistakes are dealt with with excessive punishment or destructive criticism, children may develop a fear of failure or low self-esteem, which can negatively affect their behavior.

The emotional support children receive at home is also critical to their behavior. Children who feel heard, understood, and supported in their home environment tend to have more balanced and positive behavior. They know they can turn to their parents for help when they face difficulties, which gives them a sense of emotional security. However, when children do not receive this type of support, they may seek attention in less healthy ways, such as acting out or defiantly to get their parents' attention.

In conclusion, the home environment has a profound and lasting influence on children's behavior. Parents play a central role in modeling behaviors, setting rules, and providing emotional support. A home environment that fosters stability, love, and open communication creates the ideal conditions for children to develop positive and healthy behaviors. In contrast, a home where inconsistency, conflict, or lack of support prevails can lead to challenging or problematic behaviors. By being aware of how the home environment influences their children, parents can take steps to create an environment that promotes their children's emotional well-being and positive development, giving them the tools necessary to face life's challenges in a healthy and successful manner.

Fostering Autonomy in Children

Fostering autonomy in children is one of the most valuable gifts we can offer them as parents. Autonomy gives children the ability to trust in their abilities, make decisions, and solve problems on their own. Although as parents we sometimes have the tendency to want to do everything for our children so that they don't face difficulties, it is essential to allow them to explore the world and learn to do things on their own. Autonomy not only helps them develop confidence, but it also strengthens their sense of responsibility and teaches them to deal with the consequences of their decisions.

From a very early age, children begin to show signs of wanting to do things for themselves. This is a natural and healthy process in their development, but it can be difficult for parents to see their children struggling with tasks that we could do for them in a heartbeat. However, it's important to resist the temptation to jump in too quickly. Allowing children to experiment and learn through trial and error is a crucial part of the learning process. For example, when a child is trying to dress themselves and gets a knot in their shoes, it may be easier and quicker for us to figure it out. But if we instead give them time and guidance to do it on their own, we're giving them the opportunity to develop motor and problem-solving skills, plus a great sense of accomplishment when they finally get it right.

Encouraging autonomy doesn't mean that children should do everything alone or without supervision. Rather, it's about providing them with opportunities that are appropriate for their age and developmental level, and being there to support them when they need it. At first, this may involve simply allowing them to choose their own clothes or decide what game to play. As they get older, they may take on larger responsibilities, such as helping with household chores or managing their time more independently. The important thing is that parents provide the necessary support, but also the space for children to take initiative and develop their own confidence.

One of the keys to fostering autonomy is offering them choices. When children have the opportunity to choose from a variety of options, they feel like they have some control over their environment and their lives. This can be as simple as allowing them to choose between two or three options of clothes to wear in the morning, or asking them what activity they prefer to do in their free time. When children are empowered to make decisions, they begin to develop a sense of responsibility and learn to think for themselves. In addition, giving them choices within reasonable limits teaches them to make informed decisions, consider consequences, and develop their judgment.

Another important aspect of fostering autonomy is setting clear expectations. Children need to know what is expected of them, but they also need the freedom to meet those expectations in their own way. For example, if we ask them to clean their room, rather than telling them exactly how to do it step by step, we can give them general guidelines and allow them to find their own method. They may not do it the way we would do it, but the goal is for them to learn to be organized and make decisions about how to complete the task. As they practice, they will get better at carrying out these responsibilities.

It's also important to teach children to accept the consequences of their actions, both positive and negative. When we allow them to make choices, we also teach them that those choices have results. For example, if they decide not to pick up their toys after playing, a logical consequence might be not finding their favorite toy the next time they look for it. This isn't about punishment, but about helping them understand that their actions have an impact on their environment. As they experience the consequences of their choices, children learn to make more informed choices and be more responsible.

Another crucial point in promoting autonomy is avoiding perfectionism. As parents, we sometimes want our children to do everything "correctly" or "perfectly," but it's important to remember that they are learning. Perfectionism can inhibit autonomy, as children may feel like they can't do anything well enough and therefore prefer not to try at all. Instead of focusing on whether the job they did is perfect, we should celebrate effort and progress. If a child tries to make their bed for the first time and it doesn't come out perfect, instead of correcting them or doing it ourselves, we can praise them for trying and gently guide them to do better next time. In this way, we encourage a growth mindset, where effort and learning are more important than the end result.

Patience is a key tool when it comes to fostering autonomy. Sometimes, letting a child do something on their own can take longer and require more effort than if we did it ourselves. However, it is important to remember that this extra time and effort is an investment in their long-term development. Over time, children who have had the opportunity to do things on their own develop problem-solving skills, self-efficacy, and confidence in their own abilities, which better prepares them to face life's challenges.

Emotional support also plays a big role in autonomy. Children need to know that even though they are encouraged to do things on their own, they always have the support and guidance of their parents if things get difficult. This support doesn't mean solving all their problems for them, but rather being there to provide guidance when they need it. If a child is trying to build something with blocks and gets frustrated, instead of taking the blocks and doing it for them, we can ask them what they think they could do differently to make it work, or give them a small suggestion that guides them to the solution. This way, the child knows that they are not alone, but that they are still capable of solving the problem on their own.

It's also important to acknowledge and value children's achievements, no matter how small. When a child manages to do something on their own, such as getting dressed, making a sandwich, or completing a school assignment without help, it's crucial to acknowledge that achievement. This reinforces the idea that they are capable and competent, and motivates them to keep trying in the future. A simple "You did great!" or "I'm proud of how you managed to do that on your own" can have a huge impact on their confidence and motivation to continue being autonomous.

Autonomy also helps them develop healthy self-esteem. When children feel capable of doing things for themselves, their self-esteem grows. They know that they are capable of facing challenges and solving problems, which gives them a sense of control over their own lives. Additionally, autonomous children are more likely to take the initiative in different situations, which prepares them to be independent and self-confident adults.

In short, fostering autonomy in children is a process that requires time, patience, and constant support. By allowing them to make decisions, take responsibility, and experience the consequences of their actions, we are giving them the tools necessary to grow into confident, responsible, and capable individuals. As parents, our role is to guide them, provide a safe environment where they can experiment and learn, and celebrate their achievements as they develop their independence. Autonomy not only prepares them to face life's challenges, but also gives them the confidence to believe in their own skills and abilities, which is critical to their long-term personal and emotional development.

Boosting Academic Performance

Boosting children's academic performance is a goal that many parents set themselves, but often they don't know where to start. When we talk about academic performance, we're not just referring to the grades a child gets in exams, but to their ability to learn, understand and enjoy the educational process. Success at school depends not only on the hours a child spends in front of books, but also on the environment at home, emotional support and appropriate study techniques. The key is to find a balance between learning and emotional well-being, because a motivated child who feels safe and valued will always perform better.

The first thing we need to consider is creating an appropriate environment for study. The place where children do their homework and study has a direct impact on their ability to concentrate and learn. A quiet, well-lit space, free of distractions and with everything they need within reach is ideal. It's not about having a perfect office, but rather a place where the child can focus without constant interruptions. Screens, such as the television or cell phone, should be kept away during study time, as they can break concentration. In addition, it is useful for the child to have a study routine, that is, a fixed schedule every day to dedicate time to their homework. This creates a habit, and well-formed habits are one of the bases of academic success.

In addition to space and routine, it is important for parents to be involved in their children's education, but in a balanced way. It is not about doing their homework, but about being available to answer questions and offer support when necessary. Many times, children get frustrated because they feel they do not understand a subject and do not know who to turn to. Having a parent or guardian who is willing to explain a concept or help find the answer can make a big difference. It is not necessary to be an expert in all subjects, but what is vital is to show interest in what the child is learning and to let them know that they are not alone in the process.

Motivation plays a crucial role in school performance. Children who are motivated to learn, who find meaning in what they are doing, tend to do better academically. But how can we motivate children? It is not just about offering rewards for good grades, although recognizing achievement is always positive. Rather, it is about helping the child discover the value of learning itself. For example, if a child is learning math, instead of focusing solely on getting good grades, we can show them how math is useful in everyday life, whether it is counting money, cooking, or playing a video game. By connecting learning to real, meaningful experiences, the child begins to see that what they are learning has a purpose beyond school.

Another important aspect is organization. A child who knows how to organize his or her time and materials tends to be more efficient in his or her studies. Helping children plan their tasks, prioritize what is most important, and divide large projects into small, achievable goals is essential to reduce stress and improve performance. At first, parents can guide this process, but as the child grows, it is important for them to learn to do it themselves. Using calendars, to-do lists, or even apps designed for organization can be a big help. Additionally, teaching them to divide study time into blocks with small breaks in between (known as the Pomodoro technique) can improve their concentration and productivity.

Nutrition and rest are other factors that we often overlook when we think about school performance, but they are essential. A child who does not get enough sleep or does not have a balanced diet will hardly be able to perform at his or her best in school. The brain needs energy and rest to function well, and a tired or poorly nourished child will have trouble concentrating and retaining information. It is important to ensure that children get the necessary hours of sleep and that they have a diet rich in fruits, vegetables, proteins and healthy carbohydrates. It is also useful to limit the consumption of sugar and processed foods, as these can negatively affect the ability to concentrate.

Reading is a powerful tool for improving academic performance. Children who read frequently tend to have better reading comprehension, which in turn facilitates learning in all areas. Reading not only enriches vocabulary, but also develops analytical skills and stimulates the imagination. It is important for parents to encourage the habit of reading from an early age. This does not mean forcing children to read complicated or boring books, but rather helping them find readings that interest and excite them. It can be an adventure series, comics, fantasy stories or any topic that sparks their curiosity. The important thing is that they enjoy the process and feel motivated to continue reading.

When it comes to managing school stress, it's crucial to teach children how to deal with pressure in a healthy way. As they grow older, academic expectations increase and, in many cases, children may feel like they're not up to par. It's important for parents to teach their children that it's okay to make mistakes and that learning is a process that takes time. Reinforcing the idea that effort is more valuable than perfection will help them reduce anxiety and face challenges with a more positive attitude. Relaxation techniques, such as deep breathing or mindfulness, can also be helpful for children to learn to calm down and focus during times of stress.

One aspect that we must not forget is the emotional development of the child. Self-esteem and self-confidence play an important role in their school performance. Children who believe in their abilities tend to try harder and persevere even when faced with difficulties. As parents, it is important to provide genuine and specific praise that reinforces effort and progress, rather than just the result. For example, instead of saying "You are so smart," it is better to say "I love how hard you tried to solve that problem." This helps the child understand that effort is what really counts and that they are capable of overcoming challenges.

Finally, it is crucial for parents to maintain open and honest communication with teachers. Being aware of a child's academic progress, knowing their strengths and areas of opportunity, and working together with the school can make a big difference. Teachers are a valuable source of information and guidance, and maintaining a collaborative relationship with them allows any problems to be identified early and appropriate solutions to be found.

In conclusion, boosting children's academic performance is not just about helping them get good grades, but about creating an environment that fosters a love of learning, organization, time management, and emotional well-being. With a balanced approach, parents can help their children develop the skills necessary to succeed in school and, more importantly, enjoy the process of learning.

The Role of the Father as a Role Model

The father's role as a role model is one of the most important aspects of raising children. From the moment they are born, children begin to observe, imitate and learn from the people around them, especially their parents. Although it may not seem like it at times, children pay a lot of attention to what we do, much more than to what we say. Therefore, as parents, we must be aware that our actions, words and attitudes directly influence the development of our children, how they perceive the world and how they see themselves.

When we talk about being a role model, we're not saying that parents should be perfect or should never make mistakes. We're all human and have moments when we don't act in the best way. However, what's important is that children see that their parents are trying hard to be consistent with the values they preach. For example, if we tell a child that it's important to be honest, but then they see us lie in an everyday situation, the message they receive is contradictory. Instead, if they see us being truthful even in difficult times, they will learn the value of honesty in an authentic way.

One of the first things children notice in their parents is how we handle our emotions. If we are patient, calm, and able to handle stress in a healthy way, children will learn to do the same. Conversely, if we consistently react with anger or frustration, they might imitate that behavior when they face their own problems. It's not about hiding our emotions or pretending that everything is okay, but about showing them that it is possible to face difficulties with calm and self-control. It's natural to have bad days, but when children see that we are able to pick ourselves up and move forward in a positive way, they are learning a valuable lesson about resilience.

Another area in which parents serve as role models is in the way we treat others. Children learn a lot about interpersonal relationships by watching how we interact with other people, whether at home, with friends, or in public. If parents show respect, empathy, and courtesy toward others, children will develop those qualities as well. For example, if they see us treating our friends and family with kindness and consideration, or helping someone in need, they will begin to understand the importance of kindness and cooperation. Likewise, if they witness conflict or tension, it is also important for them to see how we handle those situations, seeking peaceful and constructive solutions.

When it comes to habits and routines, parents also play a crucial role. Children tend to imitate their parents' habits, whether it's in relation to food, exercise, organization, or even technology use. If a parent has healthy habits, such as exercising regularly, eating well, or reading frequently, children are likely to follow that example. But if a child sees their parents spending long hours in front of the television or cell phone without interacting, that behavior is likely to be replicated. Similarly, if a parent values family time and dedicates specific moments to be with their children, they will learn to value those interactions and understand the importance of the family bond.

The father's role as a role model also includes teaching the value of effort and perseverance. Children need to see that success is not always immediate and that achieving goals requires dedication and work. This is best learned when parents share with them their own challenges and achievements, and show them how perseverance and patience are essential. When children see their parents strive to improve at something, whether at work, a personal project, or any other area of life, they understand that failure is not the end, but rather an opportunity to learn and grow. This is a powerful message that will help them face their own challenges with a more positive and determined attitude.

In many cases, parents are also the first role model of authority that children encounter. It is through this relationship that children begin to understand the importance of rules, boundaries, and respect for authority figures. However, the way we exercise our authority also influences how our children will understand and respond to rules in the future. If we as parents are authoritarian, strict, and controlling, children may rebel or feel insecure. On the other hand, if we show authority based on mutual respect, communication, and understanding, our children will learn to respect rules without feeling oppressed, and they will see that authority is not something that is imposed, but something that is earned.

Responsibility is another core value that parents pass on to their children through example. Children should see that their parents are responsible, not only in their work, but also in their daily lives, in the way they keep their commitments and how they take charge of difficult situations. When a child sees their parents taking responsibility for their actions, even when they are wrong, they learn a valuable lesson about the importance of being responsible in their own lives. This also includes being responsible for our words and promises. Keeping what we say is essential to building trust with our children. If we promise something, it is important to keep it, and if for some reason we cannot do so, we should explain it to them honestly.

Parents are also role models of integrity for their children. Integrity is the ability to act according to our principles, even when no one is looking. Children need to see that their parents are consistent with what they say and do, and that they act according to their values at all times. This means that we must be honest, both with ourselves and with others, and maintain our principles even in difficult situations. Children who grow up in an environment where integrity is valued tend to develop a strong sense of right and wrong, which will help them make ethical decisions in their lives.

A father's role as a role model doesn't end in childhood; it's an ongoing process. As children grow older, they continue to observe and learn from their parents, even if they don't always express it. Adolescence, for example, can be a period when children appear to distance themselves from or challenge parental authority, but in reality they continue to pay attention to what their parents are doing. At these stages, it's especially important for parents to continue to model mature, thoughtful, and understanding behavior. While teenagers may seem more independent, they still need guidance and role models to help them navigate the challenges of this stage of life.

In short, the father's role as a role model is one of the most influential factors in a child's life. It's not about being perfect, but about being aware that our actions speak louder than our words. Through our attitudes, habits and behaviors, we are teaching our children how to face life, how to relate to others and how to handle the challenges that come their way. By being a good role model, we are not only guiding our children, but also contributing to their development as responsible, empathetic and self-confident individuals.

www.ingramcontent.com/pod-product-compliance
Lightning Source LLC
Chambersburg PA
CBHW031419150726
47989CB00002B/715